MY WORDS, OUR INTERPRETATION

Poetry by
MALACHI GABRIEL

MY WORDS, YOUR INTERPRETATION

Poetry by
MALACHI GABRIEL

T&J Publishers

A SMALL INDEPENDENT PUBLISHER WITH A BIG VOICE

Printed in the United States of America by
T&J Publishers (Atlanta, GA.)
www.TandJPublishers.com

© Copyright 2017 by Malachi Gabriel

All rights reserved. This book or parts thereof may not be reproduced in any form, stored in a retrieval system, or transmitted in any form by any means-electronic, mechanical, photocopy, recording, or otherwise-without prior written permission of the author, except as provided by United States of America copyright law.

Cover design by Timothy Flemming, Jr. (T&J Publishers)
Book format and layout by Timothy Flemming, Jr. (T&J Publishers)

ISBN: 978-0-9981621-4-0

To contact author, go to:
www.malachigabriel.com
infomalachigabriel@gmail.com
instagram: @therealmalachigabriel

Acknowledgments

I would like to give thanks to God for helping me in my battle with addiction and depression for the past decade. I would like to thank Him for giving me the strength to get through my struggle and this book. I am grateful to Him for being there in my darkest days and troubled times.

This book is dedicated to those who are battling with addiction, depression, and facing other personal struggles. If you stay positive and keep striving for victory, you can overcome whatever problem(s) you are going through.

I would like to thank Angel for encouraging me when I needed it. From our midnight drives to our video chats, you always made me laugh and kept me entertained. I would like to thank you for proofreading and editing this book along with your sister, Ashley. You were always there to listen to my problems and, God knows, I had a lot of problems; but you always put me in a good mood.

I would like to thank my mentor, Mr. Matthew Curtis, for teaching me biology my freshman and senior year in high school. You also taught me about life and gave me life lessons that I will carry on and live by and pass on to my kids. No matter what crazy job I want to pursue, you are there to help me plan out the road on how I am going to get that job and be successful.

I would like to thank Marcus, Moise, and Karlynski for telling me to find and pursue my passion, for giving me little nuggets of wisdom from time to time, and for telling me to forget about trying to make money. You guys told me to just do what I love and the money will come.

I would like to thank Brock for influencing and encouraging me to write. You opened the doors of writing in my life. You inspired me to use writing as a tool to release stress in my life.

I would also like to dedicate this book to my nephews Cameron, Calil, Cayden, and Caleb. I know you guys are going to be successful when you get older. Just be patient and keep using your head because your time will come.

Introduction

Many people struggle with addiction in their lives; they become addicted to things in order to escape the problems they face. People turn to addictions as a stress reliever. People get addicted to many things like alcohol, drugs, sex—anything that can help them experience solitude. They will do anything to escape reality.

Once you become addicted to something, it is hard to quit it. The more you give-in to your addiction, the harder it gets to break out of it; it's a cycle of stress, relief, and euphoria; then the process repeats itself over and over again. The poems in this book deals with the battle of addiction, relapse, and the mental and emotional struggles that ensue. All of these poems come from my personal experiences. This book also deals with love, religion, faith, and suicide.

These poems are meant for you to interpret for yourself. I wrote them, but you can come up with the meanings however you see fit. Some of them might be complicated and some of them might be easy; just focus on clarifying the poems for your own benefit.

I.

As a man sitting in hell,
I wonder at what point in my life did I fail?
Was it because of the greed, envy, or lust?
Or was it because of the jealousy, hatred, or disgust?
No matter what, my body is going to end up as dust.
There is no one left to hear me fuss.
I have given up and lost all trust.
As I walk down the corridor to death
I realize I have nothing left
but to see that it is my time for death.
As I make it to my destination and sit in the Devil's chair
I become aware of the butcher that I am.
Prepare to sit in agony for eternity,
for it was I who pulled the trigger that
killed your descendant.
I ask for no mercy
as I am ready to sleep with death
and disappear from this life where I have made a mess.

2.

As a person who takes away life,
I yearn for the day that my life will be taken away.
Where will I go anyway?
Will I go to the land of happiness
or the land of despair?
Where did my prey go?
Did some go upwards or downwards?
If I turn my life over to Yahweh,
is there a chance that
I can see my victims in the land of freedom?
The followers of Yahweh said
if I am truly sorry for my wrongdoings
then I can be forgiven.
Does that mean my evil acts will go away for eternity?
If that is true then will the relatives of my victims
be angry if they see me in paradise with their loved ones?
Would they stop believing?

3.

I watch the kids I share my knowledge with
go on with their lives to become strong-minded individuals;
however, some become weak-minded and go down dark paths,
which makes me question,
Should I have done more for those kids?
Should I have been a better master for my pupils?
Or was it their wrongdoings that led them
down their dark roads?
All I can do is watch their lives fade away.
Sometimes, I feel like I should go help them
and steer them away from the darkness;
however, I have a new generation
that wants to learn from me.
How can I help someone who doesn't want my help
while helping someone who needs my help?
My pupils who chose the wrong path,
I'm sorry that I did not do a better job
in giving you my knowledge.
But to the ones that need my help,
I hope you can take my teachings
and become kings and queens of this universe.

4.

If I die without finding you, what was my purpose for living?
If I depart from this world without this feeling or emotion,
then why was I ever born—if I couldn't enjoy you?
I have experienced half of you
but not the whole thing.
I wanted the whole experience and not a little bit.
I partially had you in my life throughout my childhood and
adulthood but I really never got the chance
to see the full version of you.
I wanted you and only you.
Some people played with you and your name.
They took advantage of you.
I just wanted to be in your presence for one day.
But now that I'm shabby and fatigued,
my life is full of anger and hatred—
the opposite of your kindness—
and I don't think I will be able to face you like this

5.

At this point in my life, lust is dead to me.
I don't want you at all in my life.
I find no pleasure in partaking in any activities
that deal with you.
No matter who tells me you are fun and enjoyable,
you are disgusting and filthy.
I let individuals coerce me to let you fill my life up.
Now, in the present day, my body rejects you.
Hopefully, down the road I can enjoy you again
and accept you when I fuse with my counterpart.
But until then, you stay away from me.

6.

She please me with greens from the sale of her body.
Her perfume brings joy to my sense of smell.
The smooth skin of her figure
melts my pockets cause I know I will have a good sale.
Every corner spot will be glowing
with that *thang* on the streets.
Better than dope; better than booze.
This mean *burner*—it's the new heat.
I treat her right; she treats me well.
I'm the only one that truly cares
if she's hot or not,
because if she's not then just like that she gets dropped.
My lavish words are powerful
to her developing mind.
If I want, she can be dead by her own hands
or she can be larger than life without no man
because that's how the soothing tone
of my smooth vocals work.
It's not a weapon that can take her from you,
but a man's spiritual flavor in his speech
that can make her leave you.
Now, welcome to my world of adventures
and sumptuous destinations.

7.

I want to talk to you in person.
I want to be with you everywhere you go.
You are me and I am you.
When other people talk to you
they disrespect you like you are not powerful.
I do not want to connect with you
on a mental or physical level anymore.
My life was incomplete before you.
But now, I want to be full of your hope and grace.
Some people curse in your name,
but I will never mix your name with such foul language.
Over and over, second after second,
my soul is empty from not having you in my presence.
But not anymore.
I am leaving my heart unlocked
so you can walk through the door.

8.

I am in fondness with the beautiful soul
I have become attracted to.
We have produced heavenly descendants
for us so our legacy can carry on.
We have chosen the quintessential residence for us to bask in.
We have both chosen the perfect métier
for us to live happily.
But after all of this
I feel like my life has not been perfect.
Maybe I should have chosen a better mate
that was identical to me
because I still do not love my wife.
I don't even think I was ever attracted to the opposites.

9.

As a soul taker, I wonder why He lets me do this.
I question why He lets me destroy lives.
People pray to Him,
but I eradicate them right before His very eyes.
I sometimes make them plead to Him for help
so He can save them and me;
however, He is nowhere to be found
and I finish my job as a beast to slaughter my prey.
This is who people come to when they are in trouble.
This is who people rely on when they are in need of something.
Well, forget it because death is here
to smite down your very existence
and nobody is going to rescue you.
But still, throughout my terror,
there are still people who follow Him,
including my victims, to their dying breath.
They will never curse out His name,
but I would
because He betrayed me.

10.

Day by day, my body turns to dust.
Night by night, my mind turns to rust.
I was so busy taking care of you
that you forgot to take care of me.
I did my best in life to teach you how to be successful,
now it's your turn to watch me be restful.
Instead, you throw me away.
Instead, you treat me like shit.
Instead, you make me feel like I'm less of a man.
I yearn for the day that I can rest in peace,
but you let these outsiders come and control me
like I'm a sick puppy.
No matter what I still love you
But you, too, will learn how I feel,
for it is a generational curse to forget about your predecessor
as I did and as the elder before me did.
You, too, will learn what it is like to feel dead
while you are still alive.

II.

I'm in paradise when I am around you.
You bring joy to my heart.
You bring love to my pain.
People tell me to stop.
People tell me to leave you alone.
They cannot comprehend you
or grasp your attention.
They don't understand the joy you bring to my sorrow.
Just for a moment I feel peaceful;
then, as time passes on, I am burning again,
yearning each hour for your attention
until one day you consume me into your madness
and then we can be with each other for eternity.
Everybody says I should leave you alone
because you are no good to my body;
however, you were with me in the darkest hours
and you would stay with me in my deepest troubles.

12.

Some call it a cop out;
I call it my only way out.
You battle for so long
that you feel like you can't fight it anymore.
You think about asking for help
but you think people won't understand.
You think people are going to judge you
if you ask for help.
You fight this battle for so long in the shadows
because you feel like you have it under control;
however, you never had it under control
and now you realize it.
Again, you want to ask for help
but you feel like people are truly not helping you
and are just using your pain and struggles
for their own agenda,
so you have no one to turn to but yourself.
When you don't want to fight anymore
you look to one more option to stop this battle,
Demise.

13.

You look at the stars for peace.
You listen to the quiet to relax.
You live in the dark to not be bothered,
but you only run away from the problem.
You look at your worries and cry.
You cannot hide forever.
The demons will come
every time you put them behind you.
They will resurface.

14.

Mother tells me that we get to light some candles tonight
and that we should keep the lights off tonight.
She really does not want me to flip the light switch up.
Mother said,

"We are going to eat some sandwiches with some
Mrs. Butterworth."

I love it when she prepare these meals for me;
however, tonight she is weeping very quietly
so I do not hear.
But I do hear although I do not understand
why is she crying?
I'm here! Am I bad? Did she get a call from my school?
Why is she crying? Does she think the food is nasty?
I love these kind of sandwiches.
Why she crying? Does she not love me anymore?

"Well, I apologize, mother, for whatever I've done," I say.
"Sweetie, I will always love you," she lovingly responds.

15.

I have not seen her yet,
but I wonder will I be the greatest thing in her world?
I wonder would she love me like she say she will?

I heard he is a tough soldier.
I heard he never ran from anything or anyone.
I know he will fight for me whenever I need help.

They were supposed to be there for me
whenever I needed them to be;
however, they weren't because they gave up on me.

16.

Always look for the light in the shadows.
You may be lost,
you may be gone,
but you can always find your way back.

17.

The smells of her fragrance brings
illustrious dreams to my thoughts.
Her sister end suffering to my pain
when they are rolled up together
when the heat arrives my soul vanishes
away with her aroma and I am married
to her through love and physical attraction.

18.

I see my reflection in her tears—
the pain I caused her year after year.
Now, I'm sitting alone again
in my chamber of reflection,
staring at myself, wondering why
I abuse the one that felt connected to me the most.
Cleansing my soul, ruining her spirit
fixing my body, damaging her foundation,
I was releasing stress, she was taking in stress.
Now, there's nothing left for me to do
but to get rid of this mess because
there is no one left for me to caress.

19.

An optimistic spirit can be kind for so long,
until the demons they are holding back burst out
and destroy the only thing that's keeping them sane.
Now, with my mind scattered in pieces,
how can I piece my humanity back together?

20.

A regressed form is a depressed form
released back into a world
that threw me away.
My apologies if I don't sound gracious enough
for being with society again,
for it was the solitude that I adapted too
so I can stay balance.

21.

Warm welcome from the sun.
A nice greeting from the moon.
Hug to the sky.
Kiss to the air.
The beauty of freedom
is all I need to let go of my sorrows.

22.

The setback added more discomfort to my flesh.
The medicine just brings euphoria for a moment
so I don't slumber perpetually.
But having death in my bed sounds better
than having pestilence in my world.

23.

Your essence of flora,
your scent of nature,
brings divinity through my body.
The celestial taste of your affection
brings my spirit back to life.

24.

The steps of lust walking towards me
in a room filled with greed
telling me I can have whatever my flesh desires.
All I got to do is give in to my temptations
to become one with the universe.

25.

The chills that run through my body
reset my mind,
helps me restart my plan to greatness over.
It helps me take a step back to look
at the wrongdoings I did in my lifetime.
Now I can go into my cubicle of excellence
and go to work.

26.

The dance with love
is the only date I look for.
The fruit of life is my only appetite.
The home of righteousness
is the only place I want to be in.
The love of a goddess
is the only thing a man can ask for.

27.

A man confined to his own isolation
can never find anything to satisfy him,
but if you give a beast a prey
then he can find pleasure in tormenting his hunt,
scarring the patsy for all of eternity
because of the assault that he had to endure in his oppression.

28.

A man stuck in silence
can go insane
knowing he will never get out his room of quietness.
A group stuck in restraint
can cause violence and insanity.
When men are reintroduced to the universe
they regress back to their minds for comfort
which can lead to two things:
death or madness.

29.

You pray to the unseen.
I pray to a statue.
You read a book.
I read scrolls.
We both know right from wrong,
so why can't we join hands and sing a song.

30.

Ancestors of oppression.
Generations of depression.
But an evolution into liberation
brought us together
as a nation.

31.

I am forgotten.
My brothers are thrown away with me.
We are put in a cycle of violence and restrictions
and we have to pray that our children
do not fall under this cycle
but into the opposite sequence
of success and freedom.

32.

Dreams of happiness falls into my mind
to escape the pain and agony
I am enduring by the hands of a friend.
Euphoria fills my thoughts
as my body is being bruised and broken.
I look up and you are nowhere to be found
but I'm supposed to worship you.

33.

Family relations tore us apart.
Color made us different.
But our love for each other
makes us the same.

34.

I am raised to pursue something
that doesn't feel right to me.
I am taught a religion
that has not gave me anything.
I am supposed to relate to another sex
that I don't feel attracted to.
Can I just live? Can I be me?

35.

The legacy I want to leave behind
is something I strive for everyday.
I need greatness to be passed down
    from generation to generation.
I need prosperity in my bloodlines.
I want my descendants to have a voice.

36.

I let you tear my mind apart,
set my soul loose,
and bring pain to my body.
But now it's time for me
to reclaim what was mine
and fix the broken pieces.

37.

The screams in the darkness
is a reverb back into my entity.
For I see no light to the opening of the tunnel.
I have to search for the map from within
to escape the wasteland of my enslavement.

38.

A caged soul
is dangerous to the body,
for it has no safe environment to roam around in,
leading to wicked thoughts
when the cage door becomes unlocked.

39.

Looking at a man eyes
you can see the wasteland he's been through,
you can see the people he harmed,
you can see so much and wonder,
'How can a man survive through so much?'
Then you stop looking at yourself in the mirror.

40.

The mind of lust is a scary place to be.
You forget about love and passion.
Wicked thoughts and foolish acts take over.
They control what a man say and do.
If you get stuck in this place,
it's hard to find your way back to peace.

41.

The effects of war can drain a man.
He can lose strength in his mind and body,
So much that he has to look for poison
to fix his needs
and be raptured into a state of glee.
Just give the man the help he desires
and not judge him for his struggles.

42.

The presence of meditation
brings patience back into your life.
It brings your mind back to a stop
the universe of life.
It's a wonderful thing.
And if you don't stop to see
what the world got to show you
then you can miss a glorious chance
that was meant for you.

43.

The actions a beast take to satisfy his hunger are deadly.
The route he will go to quench his thirst is alarming.
For he has loss of empathy towards humanity.
Feelings are not present in his mind anymore.
Remorse and guilt are nowhere to be found.
The only thing a beast focuses on is pleasing his needs.

44.

Rinsing the dirt off your body
does not take away the pain
the world caused you.
The dirt is imprinted on you.
It's hard to clean something that stays rotten.
Your soul is infested with demons
that want you to destroy yourself.

45.

I sit on the bench
waiting for Mother Nature's daughter to arrive
and take me up with her love and courage.
Our affair will feel like
I'm in paradise again.

46.

The treasure of potential
is a lost profit.
A man truly does not know how gifted he is
until he is shown the power
that he holds within himself
to make his own destiny.

47.

Calling Death is the conclusion I had come to.
I called life and happiness,
but it went straight to voice-mail.
I wonder do they know that they have missed calls from me?
However it does not matter anymore,
for I am ready to sleep with peace for eternity.

48.

If you listen to a regular man,
he can show you how to be standard.
If you listen to a knowledgeable man,
he can show you how to be wise.
If you listen to a smart man,
he can show you how to be intelligent.
If you listen to a foolish man,
he can take you down foolish paths.
Choose the right man to listen to
or choose the right man to follow.

49.

I gave you power
because no one gave me anything.
I gave you my wisdom
because no one shared theirs with me.
I gave you my love because
I wanted you to feel to love.
If no one gives you anything
then how will you share your knowledge
with your descendants?
If a man never taught you about life
then how can you become a man?

50.

A broken heart.
A lost soul.
Negative remarks.
No control over your life.
But always focus on the burning candle
because that's your only light.

51.

The mind of a child is a beautiful thing,
but at the same time dangerous,
for it can be turned into evil and darkness.
The child needs a savior to guide him
to make sure his mind, body, and soul
be wise enough to guide and impact
the generation after him.

52.

Looking at the body of a soulless man—
a man lost for empathy,
lost for love—
you wonder how you can save him.
How can you save yourself?

53.

An underlying depression
can drive a man to suicide,
For he doesn't know what is driving him to loneliness.
War with demons,
losing battles,
can cause a man to give up,
but help from friends and love
can give a man triumph over his struggles.

54.

We are so focus on closing doors,
locking doors, and throwing away the key
to all our problems.
Why don't we just leave the door open,
walk into the room and clean it up
instead of trying to leave the pain?
Fix the pain.
Ease your mind and remove the torment.

55.

Washed away pain with laughter;
a happy person with a broken soul;
cheer you up but can't bring joy to himself;
all he can do is just hope for the best.

56.

Seeing you become somebody is all I need
even if I become dirty and unsuccessful.
Seeing you being a productive member of society,
being a ruler amongst men,
will bring tears of joy to my eyes.

57.

When heaven rises,
hell will fall.
If you go to war with those that oppose your success
you will prevail.

58.

Your words ease my pain.
When my mind is cloudy
and filled with rain,
you know what to say to turn the tide in my brain.

59.

Destined for greatness;
looking at the stars;
looking at my future;
looking at my success;

however, I still do not know
how to get there.

60.

I'm so good at being a disappointment.
I should just quit at life and make this a job.
But my heart and soul don't want me to stop.
They tell me to keep going.
But how can you think positivity
when all you hear is negativity?

61.

I see the bridge,
but why should I drive on it
when I can drive off it
and see where destiny will take me?

62.

The tide gets closer to my body.
The light disappears from my eyes.
I think about sleeping with the ocean everyday,
but you are in my life, finally;
and now, I must fight the evil that is against me.

63.

A cold night at the lake to clear the mind.
The water bring chills to my soul,
freezes my heart;
the cold air makes my tears drift away,
but your warmth brings me peace.

64.

A hard fought battle
can put tears on a man's body;
his enemies can make him lose focus;
the terrain and climate can make him give up on survival,
but your love can give him the last bit of strength
he needs to fight back.

65.

So many distractions. Where's the clarity?
So much hatred. Where's the love?
So much sadness. Where's the happiness?
So much violence. Where's the peace?
So many problems.
JUST LET IT GO!

66.

Your love keeps me going.
Your love tames the beasts in my cage.
Your love can bring a soul back to its lifeless body.
Your love is the reason my life has not come to a conclusion.

67.

If you speak, I will listen.
If you offer help, I will take it.
The only problem is
I don't hear or see you,
so how would I know that you trying to reach me?

68.

Your love is godly.
Your presence is heavenly.
Your mind grabs my attention.
Your lips talk to me.
Where will you be when I need you?

69.

A quiet fortress is what I need to clear my mind.
The sound of silence brings me back to an innocent mind.
The world can change a man.
Sitting in solitude feels my soul with tranquility once again.

70.

In a room full of mirrors
you do not look at yourself,
but stare at the creature that is gazing back at you.
You can see the creature's distaste for compassion.
You say that's not you;
you laugh and think that's not you;
but when you walk out that room
you would not be able to tell the difference.

71.

As a child, I grow up to please you.
As a pre-teen, memory and skills come to me.
As a teen, you teach me responsibility.
As a young adult, you teach me about love and the real world.
As a man, I take my teachings and become successful to carry on your legacy.

72.

Pressure can put strain on the mind.
Support for your agenda and not theirs
can put worries on the heart.
Pleasing you and your needs is what they strive for.
Their happiness is your happiness.
You live through them.
They do not feel anything anymore.
Stop!
Let them live, love, and have passion for themselves.

73.

Will today be the day that my light disappears?
A caged lion can never be able to enjoy life
without the taste of freedom
the animal once had in his homeland;
but after it was captured for being himself,
he lost the taste for independence,
and now yearns for a better life.

74.

The illusion in my eyes
tricks my mind into thinking that there's peace again;
however, my body still feels shattered.
So how can I enjoy something intellectually
when my flesh is cracked?

75.

As a brother, I can only help you
if you want my help.
You are not alone in your battle against iniquity.
All I got to say is just take it slow.
But my love is here for you
like it always has been.
It would never go away.
The door to my home is always open.

76.

I watched you struggle everyday.
I gave you my love
when you loss your humanity.
As your mind faded away
I was there to share mine.
You were my family
when I had no family.
So wherever you drift off to,
just save a seat for me?

77.

Water fills my eyes
as I become one with pain.
I block out those
who seek to destroy you.
I will take the abuse
if you bring us home to victory.

78.

Our destinies attract one another.
Our dreams interact with each other.
Our streams meet up at the river.
Our voices are alike.
Our thoughts are connected to one another.
Just take my hand
and walk with me to the edge of the universe.

79.

Let's put on the rings of eternity
and live in the home of nature.
Our bodies will fuse with trees.
Our soul will merge into air
and breeze through the skies.
Our minds will fuse with the animals of the jungle
and gaze through the fields of essence
while our love controls the seasons.

80.

I would love to have power over my emotions,
control the urges of my body,
turn the switches and gages on
when they need to be turned on;
however, I am a broken man.
My appeal is not the same as other men.
My love is dangerous to a world of hypocrites.
My feelings are sins and my spirit is wicked.
Enemy to my own family;
outsider to my religion.
What do I have to do to change myself,
to be accepted once again in society?
DIE!

81.

The pity of the world
is what a weak-minded individual depends on.
The faith of destiny
is what a strong-minded individual lives on.
Belief in one's self
is all that a person needs to get himself to the top.
No belief, no goals.
No goals, no success.
No success, no life.

82.

I am captured, beaten, and thrown away.
I am beaten, thrown away, and captured.
I am thrown away, captured, and beaten.
No matter how you put it,
I live through it every day in this society.
My spirit is captured with the evils of the world,
body and mind are beaten everyday,
and my love is thrown away.
This is just the pain that I had become numb to
just to survive during this time of war and desperation.

83.

My reflection looks at me in disgust,
curses at me,
and then walks away from me,
leaving me to look at a blank canvas
of embarrassment.
Staring at a scene of defeat,
my life would be complete
if I just stop the non-sense
and focus on the appearance that matters the most,
my mind.

84.

As a child of violence,
I must reciprocate the actions I see.
Living in a jungle,
I must behave in a crude manner;
to survive,
punish those who hurt me.
Even though I know
violence does not beget violence,
I cannot accept that;
for I will kill those
that killed my childhood.

85.

I am abused but not broken.
I am hurt but not injured.
I am left behind but not forgotten.
I am killed but not dead.
You can't destroy a soul
that's already in heaven.
You can just watch in agony
as they prosper in luxury.

86.

The view from a minor,
it's unique;
for they do not see
Black or White,
right or wrong;
they just see.
They don't try to comprehend the situation;
they just live in the moment.

87.

The sound of love covers my spirit,
takes me on a journey through space and time
where my fantasy is my reality.
My body is wrapped up in ecstasy.
I do not feel any discomfort to my mind.
My depression has left my world of defeat.
I am feel with intoxication of jubilation and glee.

88.

Imagination rules the mind;
abstract thinking makes a beautiful spark
in the head that leads to
impossible ideas
or ideas that a regular human
can't see themselves pursuing.
You have to be and think complex
to do the abnormal.
Change the world
before it changes you.

89.

A flawed attribute in my character
makes my beliefs hollow.
Secrets of your own;
yet, you judge me
because you know mine.
Well, if I was to creep around your house,
would I find a locked door?
We're all trying to stop a war
while trying to end the bloodshed in ourselves.
Let's patch each other up,
cease fire with our demons and enemies,
rebuild a better generation
that can build a new world.

90.

The violence of words
leads to the anger of actions;
can't live a life of hate
without being hated;
poisoning mentalities
as yours was poisoned;
end suffering before it begins.

91.

As a father,
you care not abandon,
you show appreciation not criticism.
Show me how to carry myself
and not to be carried.
Show me a better road,
not an alternative.
Raise me as a man,
not as an animal.
If not, I find another source.

I LIVE BY

PEACE,

LOVE,

AND

TRANQUILTY.

YOU SHOULD TOO.

THANK YOU

www.ingramcontent.com/pod-product-compliance
Lightning Source LLC
Chambersburg PA
CBHW021133300426
44113CB00006B/403